# PUMPKIN STENCILS FOR CARVING

## Halloween Patterns for Kids and Adults

Don Santi

# THIS IS HOW TO USE THIS BOOK

**1** ## Read the Introduction

After this introduction you will learn how to carve pumpkin and which pumpkins are most suitable for carving.

Find the Patterns you like to carve on a pumpkin.

## Find Patterns **2**

**3** ## Cut Patterns

Cut out the Patterns you like and make several incisions along the edge so that it can be glued well to the surface of the Pumpkin.

# NTRODUCTION

In this introduction you will learn how you can easily carve a Halloween pumpkin.

## Which tools do you need?

The following things are needed to carve a Halloween pumpkin:

- 1 pumpkin
- A sharp, pointed knife
- A spoon
- A foil pen

Or simply buy a pumpkin carving set from Amazon.

## Here is How to carve the perfect pumpkin:

### Step 1: Open the Pumpkin arround the stem

You have to cut a hole on the top of your pumpkin around the stem and make sure to cut a whole big enough so you can get your whole hand in there.
Grab a large spoon and start digging out all of the "guts" and seeds so you're left with a clean pumpkin inside.
Then wash any dirt off of the Pumpkin.

### STEP 2: Tape your Pattern

Tape your pumpkin pattern onto your pumpkin. Feel free to do this, if it makes taping your pattern on your pumpkin. Use ample amounts of tape (make sure your pumpkin is dry) and tape your pattern on your pumpkin.

### Step 3: Mark your Pattern

Use a "push pin" or the "pokey radial tool" that comes in most pumpkin carving tool kits to poke (every 1/8 inch or .5 centimeters) on the outline of every highlighted area of your pumpkin.
You're going to get really bored doing this, but this step is really important, don't rush it.
Once you are done poking holes around the outline of each highlighted area, you can remove the pattern and tape from your pumpkin.

### Step 4: Cut out the Pumpkin Pattern

You've removed your pumpkin pattern and tape, and now you're left with a pumpkin that's got a ton of little pin pricks in it, right?
Now, take your smallest carving saw and start cutting out the marked areas (cut right on the dots).
Take your time! Especially for small and intricate areas, you're going to want to work slowly, and make sure you don't destroy your beautiful masterpiece!

### Step 5: Preserve the pumpkin!

If you've ever carved a pumpkin before, you probably know the problem that it gets moldy!
The solution is: The Bleach, Anti Mould Spray with active chlorine. This not only moistens the pumpkin, but also kills the bacteria due to the chlorine it contains.
Once you've done that, grab a candle, and display your pumpkin! Congratulations!

# PATTERNS OVERVIEW

Note: We left some pages blank so that you can glue the Blank side on the Pumpkin.

Printed in Great Britain
by Amazon

48448543R00029